Workbook 2

Caribbean Primary Social Studies
Our Country Community

LISA GREENSTEIN

HODDER
EDUCATION
AN HACHETTE UK COMPANY

Acknowledgements

The Publishers would like to thank the following for permission to reproduce copyright material.

Photo acknowledgements

p. 4, p. 5 © Vilna Robotav 3d/Adobe Stock Photo.

Every effort has been made to trace all copyright holders, but if any have been inadvertently overlooked, the Publishers will be pleased to make the necessary arrangements at the first opportunity.

Although every effort has been made to ensure that website addresses are correct at time of going to press, Hodder Education cannot be held responsible for the content of any website mentioned in this book. It is sometimes possible to find a relocated web page by typing in the address of the home page for a website in the URL window of your browser.

Hachette UK's policy is to use papers that are natural, renewable and recyclable products and made from wood grown in well-managed forests and other controlled sources. The logging and manufacturing processes are expected to conform to the environmental regulations of the country of origin.

Orders: please contact Hachette UK Distribution, Hely Hutchinson Centre, Milton Road, Didcot, Oxfordshire, OX11 7HH. Telephone: +44 (0)1235 827827. Email education@hachette.co.uk Lines are open from 9 a.m. to 5 p.m., Monday to Friday. You can also order through our website: ww.hoddereducation.com

ISBN: 9781510480735

Cover by Marc Monés from Davila Illustration Agency

Illustrations by Vian Oelofsen

Typeset in FS Albert 15/19 by IO Publishing CC

Printed in Spain

A catalogue record for this title is available from the British Library.

Contents

How to use this book

Welcome to Caribbean Primary Social Studies Workbook 2.

This workbook is full of places for you to write and make notes,

draw, doodle, colour and decorate.

The activities here will help you learn as you work through

Pupil Book 2, Our Country Community. Here are some of the

activities you will complete throughout this workbook:

- ✓ summarise key concepts
- ✓ define key words
- ✓ complete information tables
- ✓ brainstorm ideas
- ✓ draw mind maps
- ✓ present information in a flow chart
- ✓ label a diagram

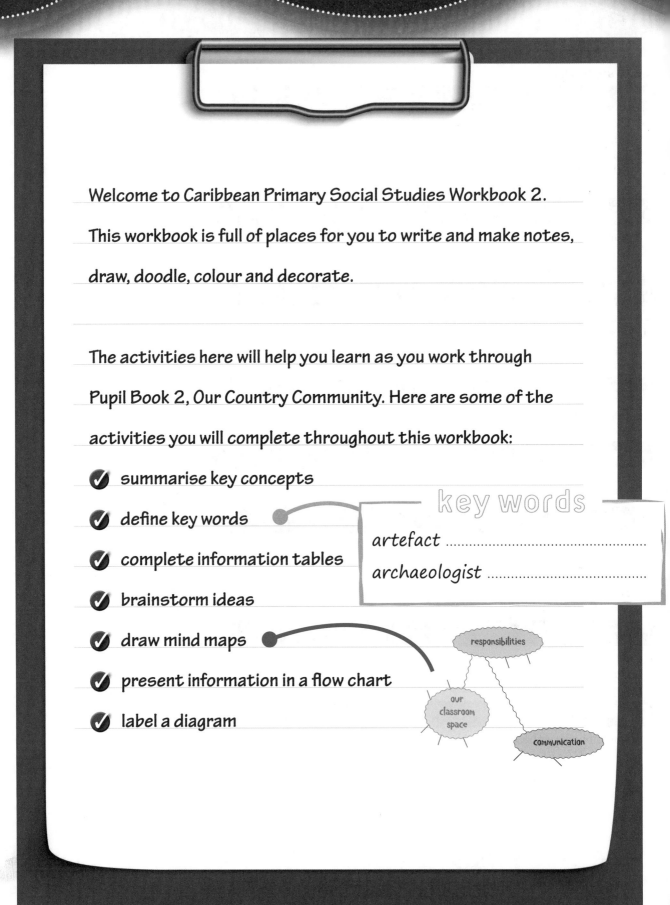

key words

artefact ....

archaeologist ....

responsibilities

our classroom space

communication

- ✅ draw a picture

- ✅ plan or record research

- ✅ draw a graph

- ✅ use a map

- ✅ write a summary

- ✅ reflect on your own experience, opinion or views on a topic.

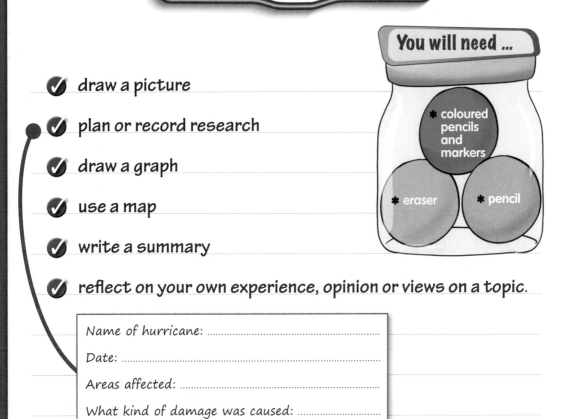

You will need ...

* coloured pencils and markers

* eraser   * pencil

Name of hurricane: ....

Date: ....

Areas affected: ....

What kind of damage was caused: ....

....

We hope you will have fun as you explore, learn and think

about your own country community.

① Brainstorm rules to include in a class code. Add your ideas to the mind map below.

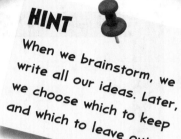

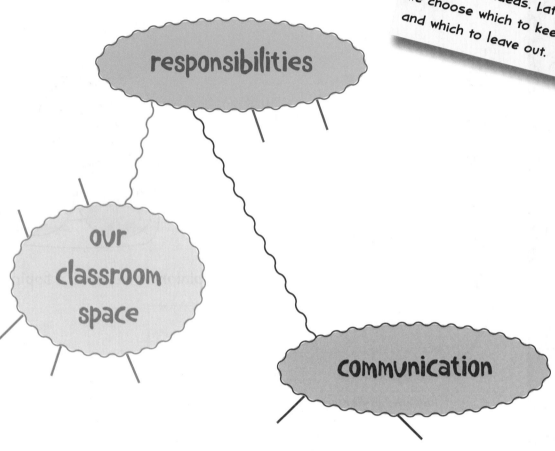

responsibilities

our classroom space

communication

② Choose five of the most important class rules, and write them in the table. Give reasons for their importance.

Class rule	Why it is important

3 Sometimes, people break rules. Breaking rules results in consequences. Discuss some of the rules your class came up with. Write three examples of rules you must follow and the possible consequences of not following these.

minor   serious   extremely serious

example			
possible consequences			

4 Explain why it is important for children to learn about rules and their importance at school.

_____

_____

_____

_____

When you join a group, you may need to complete **group membership forms**. These forms usually provide the group with your contact details and information, and give your reasons for wanting to join the group.

5 Imagine you are joining a group. It could be a sports group, a choir or a a community group – or use your imagination to make up a group! Complete the form to join the group.

GROUP NAME: _____

First name: _____ Surname: _____

Address: _____

Telephone/mobile number: _____

Email address: _____

Date of application to join the group: _____

Please give your reasons for wishing to join the group: _____

_____

_____

_____

_____

Next of kin/emergency contact: _____ Relationship to me: _____

Telephone/mobile number for next of kin: _____

I agree to abide by the rules of the group.

Signature: _____ Date: _____

6 Design a badge or symbol that your group could use.

2 Our ancestors

1 Find out more about your ancestors. Ask relatives to share what they know about your family's history. Write your family's story here and draw a picture.

Places my ancestors came from: ....

....

Why did they come here? ....

....

....

The story I found out: ....

....

....

....

....

....

....

....

....

....

1 Complete the table using information from your textbook.

	Arawaks	Caribs
Alternative name		
Building materials they used		
Things they made		
Food		
Beliefs		
Leaders		

2 Why do you think the Carib and the Arawak groups did not cooperate with each other? Imagine you were living in one of the groups. How would you feel about the other group?

_____

_____

_____

_____

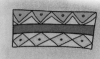

④ Other settlers

① Which countries did the European settlers come from? Unscramble the names below. Write the name of the country in the hull of each boat.

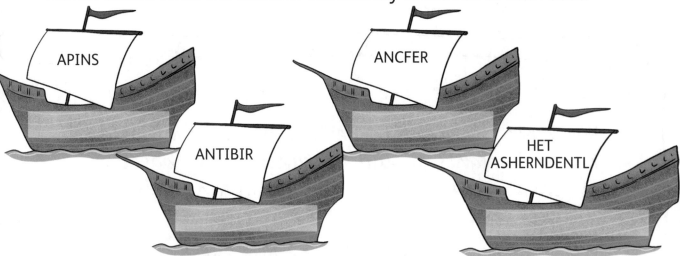

APINS

ANCFER

ANTIBIR

HET ASHERNDENTL

② What did the Europeans bring to the Caribbean?

_____

_____

③ What did the European settlers want to do in the Caribbean?

- _____

- _____

- _____

④ What caused the death of many Arawak and Carib people?

- _____

- _____

- _____

⑤ The United Nations Declaration of Human Rights is a document that declares the rights of all human beings. The first five fundamental human rights are summarised below.

✦ We are all born free and equal.

✦ We have the right to be free of discrimination. No one's rights should be taken away based on their gender, race, religion or any other differences.

✦ We have the right to life, to live safely without being in fear for our lives.

✦ We have the right to freedom from slavery, and no one has the right to enslave anyone else.

✦ We have the right to freedom from torture or slavery.

Write about how the European settlers violated all of these rights when they enslaved people from West Africa to work on their plantations.

_____

_____

_____

_____

_____

_____

_____

1 Why is it difficult to find out about people who lived very long ago?

_____

_____

_____

2 Write definitions for these key terms.

key words

artefact ....

archaeologist ....

3 Imagine that you were digging in your garden and that you found these two objects. What could the object tell you about something that happened long ago?

an old Dutch guilder, a coin that was used in the 1700s

Spanish machete (or cutlass), traditionally used as a weapon or cutting implement

4 Choose a monument or historical structure you have seen. Do research using books or the internet. Create a fact file about it. Include the name of the monument, the year it was built, the reason it was built, and what it is used for today. Also include any stories you found out about the history of the building.

_____

_____

_____

_____

_____

⑥ Names and customs

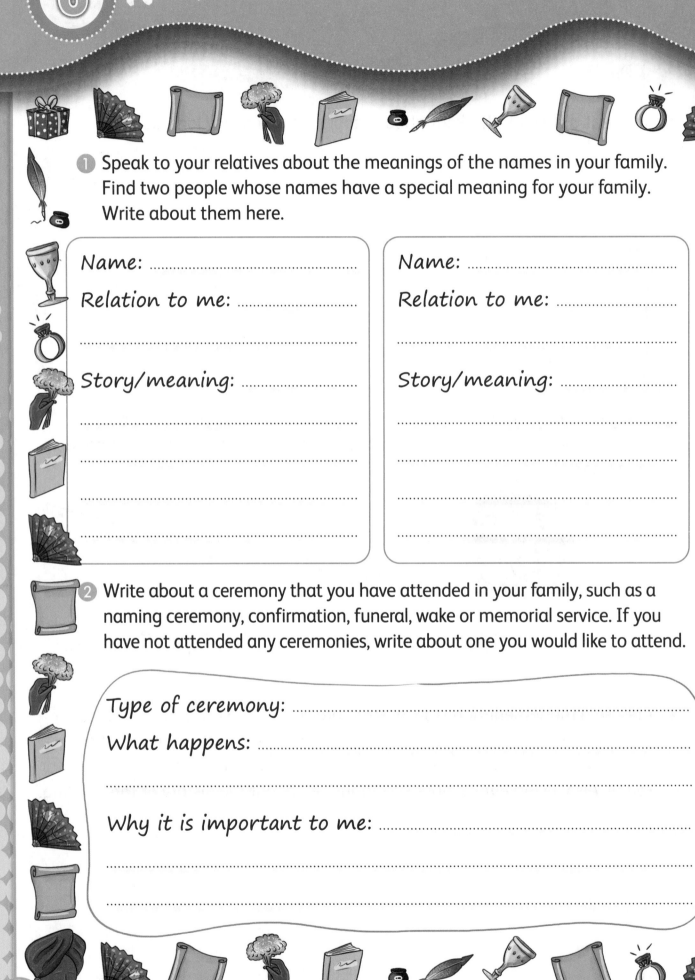

1) Speak to your relatives about the meanings of the names in your family. Find two people whose names have a special meaning for your family. Write about them here.

Name: ....

Relation to me: ....

....

Story/meaning: ....

....

....

....

....

Name: ....

Relation to me: ....

....

Story/meaning: ....

....

....

....

....

2) Write about a ceremony that you have attended in your family, such as a naming ceremony, confirmation, funeral, wake or memorial service. If you have not attended any ceremonies, write about one you would like to attend.

Type of ceremony: ....

What happens: ....

....

Why it is important to me: ....

....

....

3 Look at each picture. Write what kind of ceremony is taking place. Explain how you can identify it.

_____

_____

_____

_____

_____

_____

15

⑦ Celebrations

① Choose one of the celebrations you have read about in this unit, or choose another one that is important to you. Create a fact file below.

Name of celebration: ....

Religion or culture that it is part of:

....

Time of year that it is celebrated:

....

How long does it last? ....

Significance/meaning: ....

....

....

Special customs or practices: ....

....

....

Special foods: ....

Any special rites that mark the beginning or end of the celebration:

....

Why I like it: ....

....

....

2 Create a collage or other artwork to show the meaning, traditions and customs that are associated with your chosen celebration. You can use images, colours and words to give the sense of this special time.

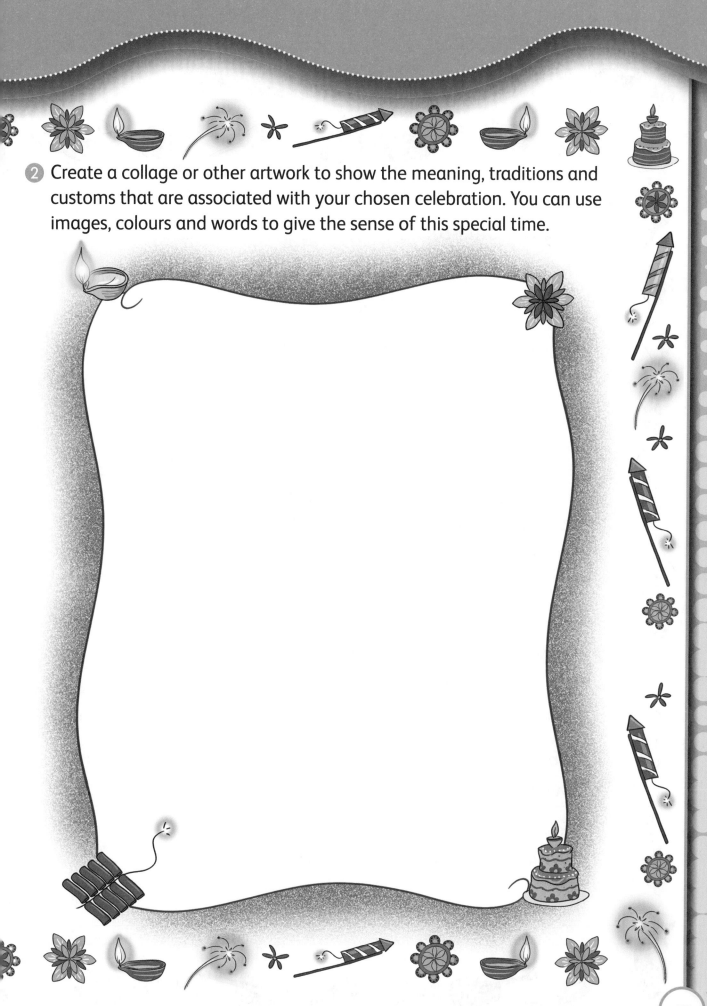

Getting to know our culture

1 Complete this paragraph about your own culture and identity.

My nationality: ....

My languages: ....

The family I belong to: ....

My religious or cultural groups: ....

....

My community groups and clubs: ....

....

Important celebrations and customs that we celebrate each year in my community:

....

....

2 Choose a writer, poet, musician or dancer from your country. Write about their work.

Name: ....

Type of artist: ....

What are they well known for? ....

....

What do you like about their work? ....

....

....

③ Imagine that you have a pen pal in another country. Write a letter or email to invite them to your country for a cultural event that you find interesting. You should include:

- when it will happen
- why you think they will enjoy it
- what they might expect to see and hear at the event
- why it is important in your country.

Dear ....

....

....

....

....

....

....

....

....

....

....

....

1 Draw and decorate a compass in the space provided.

2 Find information about your country in brochures, maps and on the internet. Draw a map of your country and put in the capital city and your village or town.

compass

10 The land and water around us

1 Is it a landform or a body of water? Tick (✔) the correct column.

Physical feature	Landform	Body of water
mountain		
river		
lake		

Physical feature	Landform	Body of water
hill		
valley		
sea and ocean		

2 Now write your own definitions.

key words

landform ....

body of water ....

relief map ....

3 Talk about the way we describe the weather. Look at the pictures below. Describe the weather conditions in each picture. Use the words from the boxes.

temperature   sunshine   rain   wind strength

wind speed   air pressure   cloud cover

4 Draw pictures to illustrate these sea conditions.

rough seas with high waves	calm sea, low tide	moderate sea, high tide

5 During the hurricane season, we use special terms to categorise the development of different weather systems. Match the correct term to the description and picture.

hurricane	tropical depression	tropical wave	tropical storm

Term	Description
	Also known as an African or easterly wave, this is an inverted trough of low pressure that moves from Africa across the Atlantic Ocean. It can develop into a hurricane.
	A type of hurricane with surface winds of up to 38 miles per hour.
	A type of hurricane with surface winds of 39 to 74 miles per hour.
	A type of hurricane with surface winds of over 74 miles per hour.

6 Find out the difference between a storm watch and a storm warning. Write what you found out below.

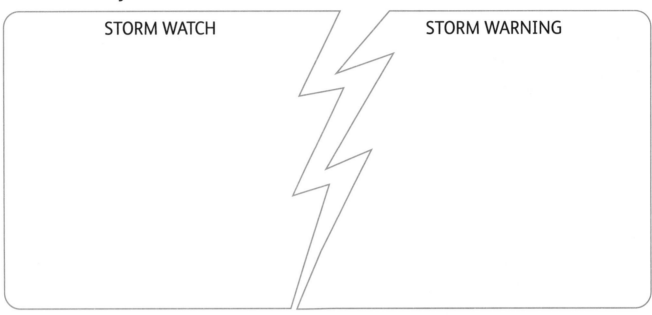

STORM WATCH   STORM WARNING

7 What are your responsibilities when there is a storm warning in your area? What can you do to keep yourself safe? Write your ideas here.

8 Research a recent hurricane that affected your area. Write your notes here.

Name of hurricane: ....

Date: ....

Areas affected: ....

What kind of damage was caused: ....

....

① Complete this worksheet with your own ideas about the different ways natural events and people change the landscape.

12 Natural disasters

① Use books or the internet to research earthquakes. Use your research to create your own notes about earthquakes.

Earthquakes

plate tectonics: _____

_____

epicentre: _____

_____

focus: _____

_____

fault line: _____

_____

Places in the world that have earthquakes often:

_____

_____

_____

How we measure earthquakes:

_____

_____

Three types of earthquakes:

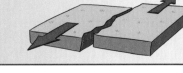

What causes an earthquake?

What kinds of damage do earthquakes cause?

2 Use books or the internet to research volcanoes. Use your research to create your own notes about volcanoes.

Volcanoes

There are four types of volcanoes:

Places in the world that have volcanoes:

ACTIVE

How volcanoes form

INACTIVE

What is a volcano?

Our natural resources

1 Look at the pictures of natural resources. For each one, decide whether it is renewable or non-renewable. Complete the table below.

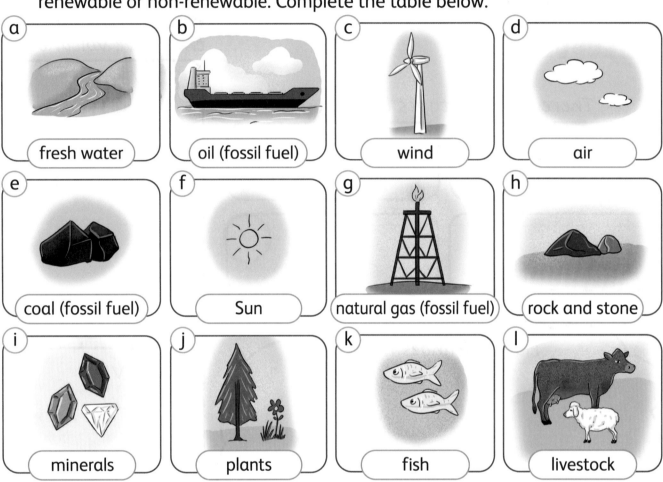

a	b	c	d
fresh water	oil (fossil fuel)	wind	air
e	f	g	h
coal (fossil fuel)	Sun	natural gas (fossil fuel)	rock and stone
i	j	k	l
minerals	plants	fish	livestock

Renewable resources	Non-renewable resources

2 When we use resources sustainably, we use them in a way that makes sure more will be available for the future. Even non-renewable resources can be overused and used up too quickly. For each of the following renewable resources, give an example of sustainable and non-sustainable use.

Resource	Non-sustainable use	Sustainable use
Fresh water (rivers and lakes)		
Fish and marine life		
Wildlife (birds, animals and insects)		
Beaches		
Forests (natural and man-made)		

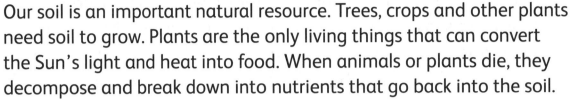

Our soil is an important natural resource. Trees, crops and other plants need soil to grow. Plants are the only living things that can convert the Sun's light and heat into food. When animals or plants die, they decompose and break down into nutrients that go back into the soil.

1 The terms below refer to things that can keep soil healthy. Do some research and write what it is, and why it is good for the soil.

Green manures

Controlled grazing

Mulch

Compost

2 Find out how to make a simple compost heap. Draw a picture with notes or instructions.

3 Each of the items below is something that damages soil. Do research and write what you found out about each term.

Chemical fertilisers	Soil erosion	Intensive tillage

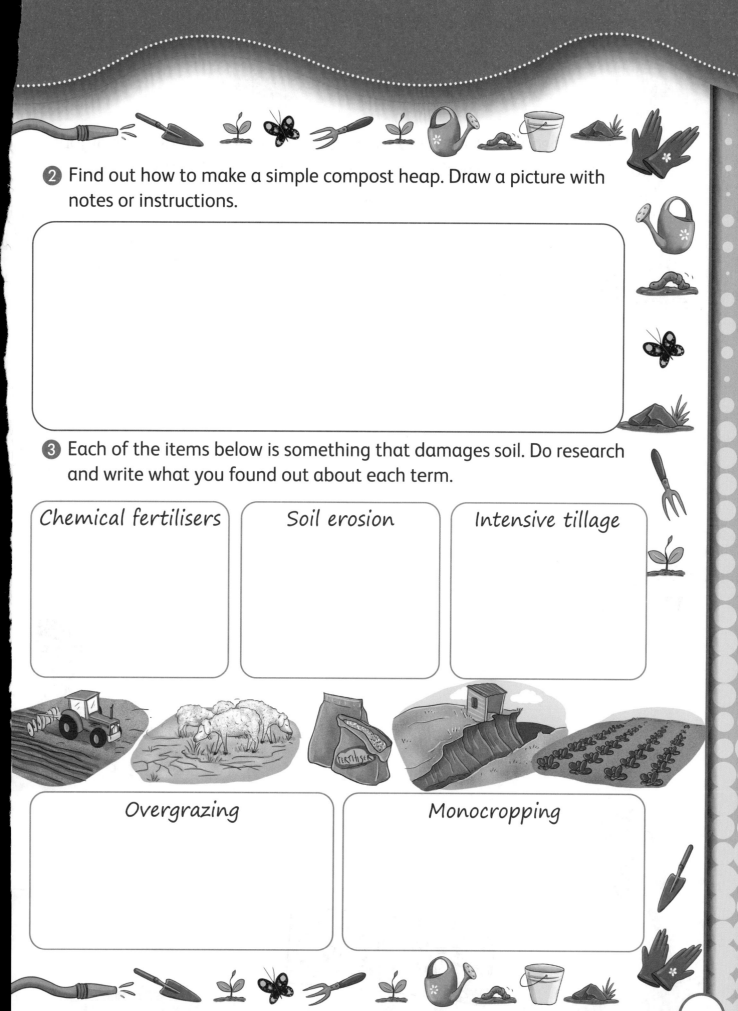

Overgrazing	Monocropping

❶ In the Caribbean, the tourist industry provides many different kinds of jobs. Brainstorm all the different kinds of work that the tourist industry provides. Use the pictures to draw a mind map.

② The pictograph below shows the number of passengers that arrived on cruise ships between January and March of one year in five Caribbean countries.

Country	Period	Number of passengers
Antigua & Barbuda	Jan–March	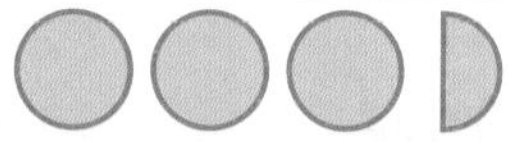 ◯◯◯◗
Bahamas	Jan–March	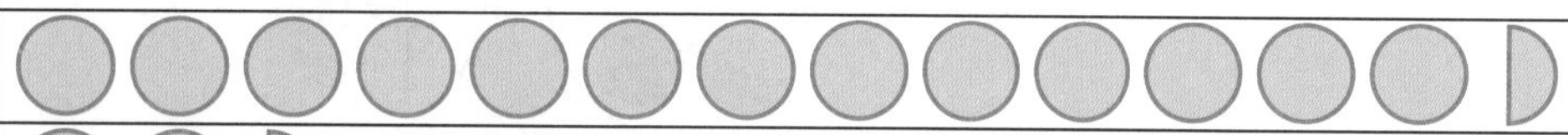 ◯◯◯◯◯◯◯◯◯◯◯◯◗
Barbados	Jan–March	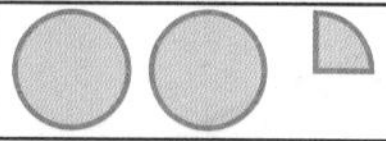 ◯◯◿
Grenada	Jan–March	 ◯◗
St. Maarten	Jan–March	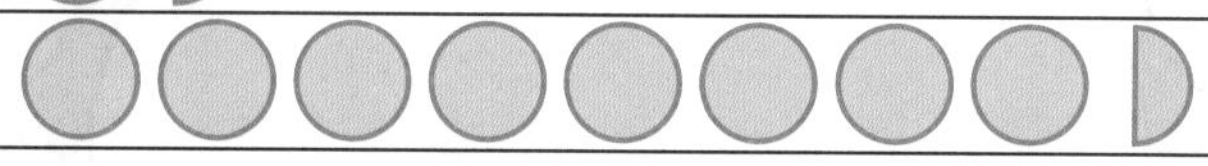 ◯◯◯◯◯◯◯◗

Key
◯ = 100 000

a Fill in the answers using the information from the pictograph.

The place with the most visitors was _____. It had about

_____ visitors between the months of _____ and

_____. The second most visited place was _____,

with _____ visitors between the months of _____

and _____. The place with the fewest visitors was

_____.

b These numbers are rounded off to the nearest 25,000.

◯ shows _____ people.

◗ shows _____ people.

◿ shows _____ people.

c Show how to draw the circles for the following figures:

St. Vincent and the Grenadines 52,219 _____

St. Lucia 399,746 _____

d Why do you think some places give their figures for 3 months, some for 4 months and some for 6 months?

_____

33

1 List the main export products of your country.

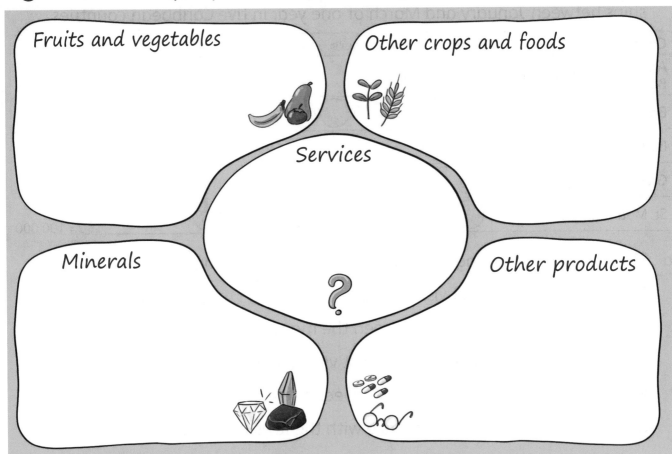

2 For each product, find out where it is exported to (both internationally and in the Caribbean).

Products of my country	Export destinations

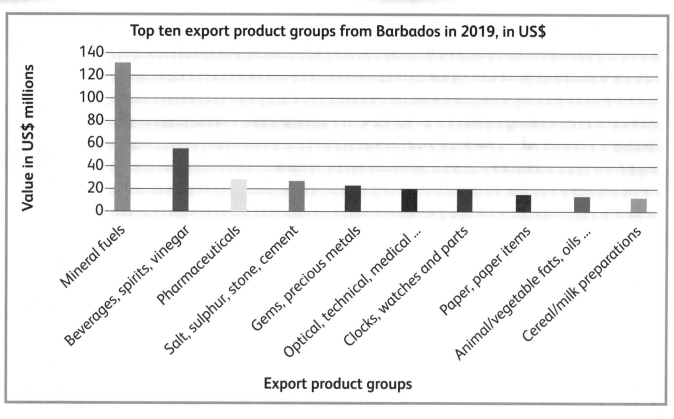

Top ten export product groups from Barbados in 2019, in US$

③ Answer the questions based on the graph.

a The group of products that brought the most money to Barbados in 2019
   was _____.

b The following groups each brought approximately $20 million into
   Barbados in 2019:

   _____

   _____

   _____

c Name three products that might fall into the category "beverages, spirits,
   vinegar":

   _____   _____   _____

④ An important function of the OECS is to ensure food security for the region.
   What do you understand by food security?

   _____

17 Travelling

In this unit, you learnt about different forms of transport. Think about the different forms of transport people use in your country. Write, draw or glue examples of each type of transport into the table.

	Private	Public
By sea		
By land		
By air		

Transportation centres

Choose a transportation centre you have used before, such as a bus station, airport or harbour. Write instructions for a visitor. Include answers to these questions:

- How can I find a timetable and the ticket prices?
- Where and how do I book the tickets? Can I book ahead?
- How early must I arrive? What must I do and where must I go?
- How much luggage can I take?
- Do I need any special documents?
- What can I expect on the trip (refreshments, entertainment, any extras)?

1 Imagine that you need to explain the rules for crossing the road to a young child. Complete the instructions here.

If possible, cross at _____

Before you cross, always _____

Wait until _____

When it's time to cross, you should _____

2 Write definitions for these key words.

===== key words =====

passport ....

immigration officer ....

customs officer ....

duty/tax ....

3 Think about the forms of transport you learnt about in Unit 17. Choose one of these forms of transport and write safety advice for using that particular form of transport.

_____

_____

_____

_____

_____

_____

_____

_____

_____

_____

_____

Before the invention of the telephone, it was impossible to communicate with your voice further than you could shout. The world's first telephone call took place in 1876.

Early telephones did not look like the mobile phones we use today. They were connected with many wires to a telephone exchange. The exchange was a huge switchboard, where people worked as operators. You had to call the operator, and they had to connect your call.

Do an internet search for 'how switchboard calls worked', and find videos to watch about how people made phone calls. Use what you find out to draw a flow diagram or cartoon showing the steps you had to follow to place a call.

1 Read what Leah's granny said about her first television.

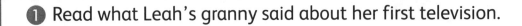

"In 1972, our family bought our first television. All the pictures were black and white. We called it 'the box', because it had a boxy design, with a tiny screen. We could watch TV in the evening. There was the news, and a few shows. You could get the daily programme in the newspaper. If we were good, our parents let us watch the children's programme at 6.30 p.m. There were no satellite TV channels and no internet or streaming like today. The only people with video cameras were TV production companies, and it was very expensive to make a show."

2 List the ways that TV has changed since then. Consider these aspects.

Who can make and record TV content

How much time we spend watching TV

Size and design

What we can watch

Channels available

3 a What do you think children spent their time doing before the invention of TV?

_____

b Why can too much TV be damaging for children?

_____

c How much TV do you think children should watch?

_____

4 TV has an **impact** on local culture. It can **influence** what we think about, what we believe and what we do. Think about things you have seen on TV that have made you want to do something, buy something or even think about something you did not know about before. Write your ideas.

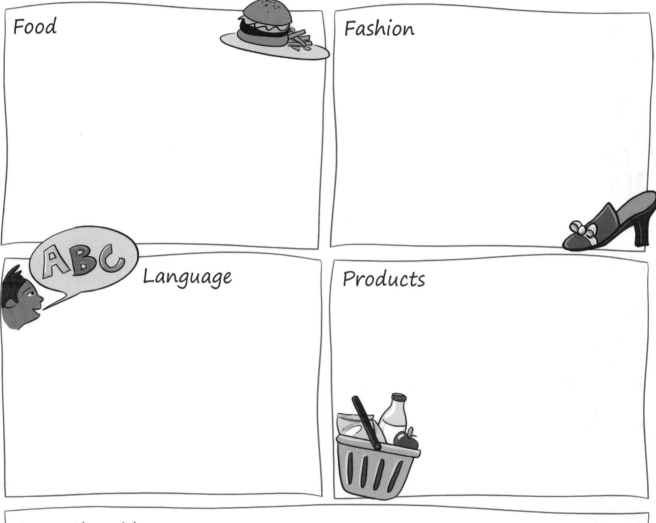

Food

Fashion

Language

Products

Any other ideas

5 What is social media? Write your ideas around this diagram showing the four main kinds of social media.

SOCIAL NETWORKING

MICROBLOGGING

VIDEOSHARING

PHOTOSHARING

6 List four **benefits** of using social media.

- _____
- _____
- _____
- _____

HINT

Benefits are things we like or find useful. For example, the benefit of exercise is that it makes you stronger. An added benefit is that it makes you feel good.

7 Choose one form of social media that you or your friends use.

Name of platform: ....

How we use it: ....

What I like about it: ....

What I do not like about it: ....

8 Technology has some benefits and also some drawbacks. Read the different statements on this page. Colour the benefits in one colour and the drawbacks in another colour. In the empty bubbles, write your own ideas.

Technology lets me chat instantly to my friend who lives in a different country.

Because of social media, I can stay in touch with family all over the world.

Sometimes when I see my friend's posts on social media, I can feel lonely and left out.

Bullying is very common on social media, as it is so easy to leave nasty comments on people's posts.

My social media accounts allow me to express myself creatively to a wide audience.

It is easy to believe false information on social media.

I can advertise my products on social media.

9 Write your own guidelines for a younger child who wants to use a social media platform.

....

....

....

1 All citizens have a responsibility to love, cherish, develop and defend our nation. Give an example of how we can demonstrate this in everyday ways.

2 What do you understand by the term 'role model'?

3 Name role models in your community, and explain what you admire about them.

④ Complete this fact file about the way your country is governed.

My country:
Form of government (pick one):

constitutional monarchy   constitutional republic

parliamentary republic

Which voting procedure best describes the country:

☐ simple majority – first past the post
☐ two-round system
☐ proportional representation
☐ other

The leader of the country, or head of state, is known as the

_____ .

Describe their main functions:

The head of the government is known as

_____ .

Who is allowed to vote in the country's general elections?

Why is voting an important responsibility?

23 Our country's leaders

Write the names of your country's leaders, including all the people elected to the parliament.

1 Complete this flow chart showing how money flows into and out of the government's Treasury.

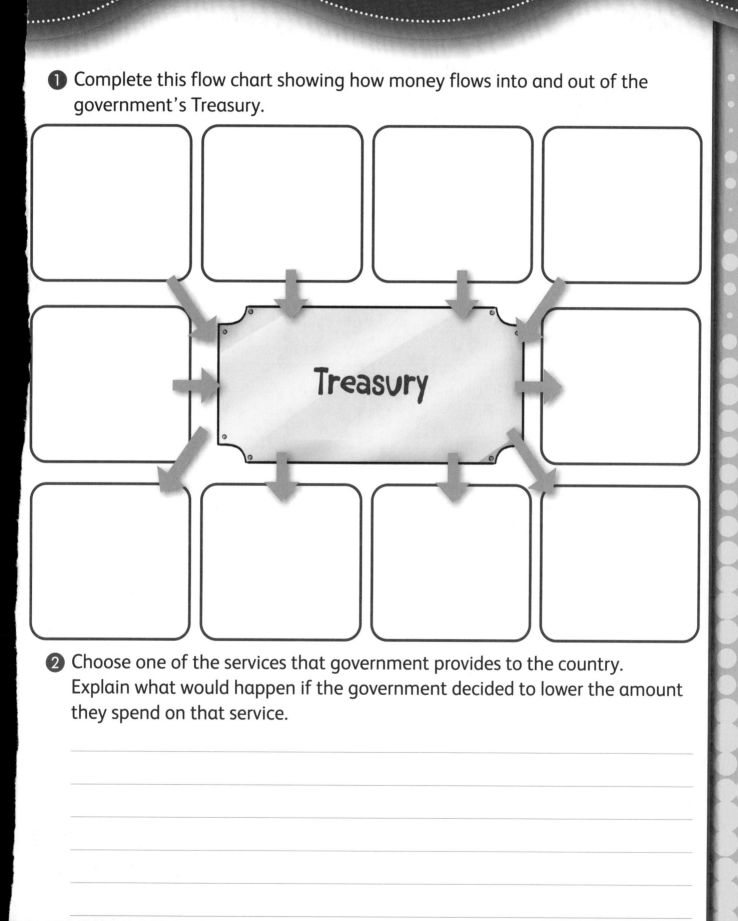

Treasury

2 Choose one of the services that government provides to the country. Explain what would happen if the government decided to lower the amount they spend on that service.

_____

_____

_____

_____

_____

_____

Choose two national symbols that are meaningful to you. Draw them, and write about what the symbol means to you.